SIMON DOBSON

JOURNEY OF THE LONE WOLF

for
Brass Band
and Percussion

SCORE

FABER *ff* MUSIC

score and parts ISBN10: 0-571-57145-X
EAN13: 978-0-571-57145-1

score ISBN10: 0-571-57146-8
EAN13: 978-0-571-57146-8

Journey of the Lone Wolf was commissioned by Dr. Nicholas Childs for Black Dyke Band,
who gave the first performance on Sunday 26 January 2014 at the Bridgewater Hall, Manchester
as part of the Royal Northern College of Music Festival of Brass.

Bartók was the Lone Wolf.
A man who musically fought tyranny and fascism.
His journey took him from the hills of the Balkans to the heart of the New World.
His singular vision may have meant a life out in the cold,
a life without warmth and love, a life without true happiness,
a death mourned by few in a strange land,
but Bartók was the Lone Wolf.

Duration: 15 minutes

To buy Faber Music publications or to find out more about the full range of titles available
please contact your local music retailer or Faber Music sales enquiries:

Faber Music Limited, Burnt Mill, Elizabeth Way, Harlow, Essex CM20 2HX England
Tel: +44 (0)1279 82 89 82   Fax: +44 (0)1279 82 89 83
sales@fabermusic.com   fabermusicstore.com

PROGRAMME NOTE

Béla Bartók (1881–1945) was one of the most influential composers of the 20th century. His work bristles with colour and energy, with its roots deep in the earth of his beloved Hungary. However, Bartók was born into a landscape of perpetual social and political change. Musically his native land was only just waking up at this point and the precocious young pianist would ultimately be its creative catalyst.

Bartók was a quiet and lonely child, prevented from playing with other children by illness after illness. He found solace in the folk music his devoted mother taught him to play at the piano. He proved to be a gifted pianist, growing into a young man whose life made sense when at the keyboard. He went on to study piano and composition at the Royal Academy of Music in Budapest, where he met Zoltan Kodály, and the pair, united by a love of folk music, became known as the first true ethnomusicologists. They would regularly take extended trips into the countryside, armed with manuscript paper and wax cylinders on which to record the traditional songs and dances. It is likely that without these records, much of the music would have been lost as political change forced the peasant and farming communities from their homes. Much of this music would later become the basis for many of Bartók's works for piano, including his famous piano method, the labyrinthine *Mikrokosmos*. Unfortunately his folk-hunting trips were cut short in 1914 by the outbreak of the First World War.

Many works from Bartók's middle period, especially his slower paced movements, have been coined "Night Music", evocative of the landscape of, or emotional reaction to, night time or darkness. He was an aloof character, alone in a vast world of change. He seemed to find very little real happiness in the company of others. Bartók did however enjoy a few close relationships, notably with his mother (whom he adored), with his first wife Marta and later with his second wife Ditta, a former piano pupil. Moments of tenderness can be heard simmering below the surface of these musical reflections.

Bartók was a staunch anti-fascist and strongly opposed Hungary's support of the Third Reich. In 1940 he was forced to flee his homeland and became exiled in the USA. He never returned home and on more than one occasion 'gave up' composing. He faced continual financial pressures but was helped to keep afloat by commissions from friends and colleagues, most notably the *Concerto for Orchestra*, his last great work. Bartók died at the age of 64 in September 1945 and his funeral was attended by only ten people. *Journey of the Lone Wolf* is portrayed in three linked movements:

1. Capturing the Peasants' Song
After the upheaval of moving to Budapest, the young Bartók meets Zoltan Kodály and the pair embark on summertime adventures through the Hungarian countryside to collect and catalogue the astonishing variety (both harmonically and rhythmically) of gypsy and folk music heard in the Balkan hills. The outbreak of the First World War plunges Bartók's beloved Hungary into chaos.

2. Night Music
Bartók was at times a cold man, aloof and lonely. The moments of tenderness he showed are portrayed here. His brief but intense affairs speak of a love he could only long for. Jazz is my "night music" and here there are hints of what Bartók may have heard in the USA in later life.

3. Flight and Fight
Having been forced by the world's evils to leave his homeland for the United States of America, Bartók, the anti-fascist, felt isolated and angry. In this movement we hear his longing for a simpler time of gypsy folk dances as well as his maturity and depth as a composer finally exploring deeper colours and darker themes.

Simon Dobson, 2014

PERCUSSION REQUIREMENTS

Revised 2016

Timpani

Percussion 1: bongos, crotales, cymbals, hi-hat cymbals, snare drum (medium high), suspended cymbal, tambourine, tam-tam.

Percussion 2: concert bass drum (shared), brake drum (shared), kit bass drum (with double kick pedal), snare drum (shared), suspended cymbal (shared), tam-tam (shared).

Percussion 3 (optional): brake drum (shared), crotales (shared), snare drum (shared), suspended cymbal (shared), tam-tam (shared).

Percussion 4: tubular bells, vibraphone, xylophone.

PERFORMANCE DIRECTIONS

Soloists are marked to stand at various points during the performance.

Vibraphone should be placed behind the repiano and soprano cornets and treated as needing to be heard (where scoring dictates) across the band.

All *legato* notes should be played as long as possible.

Instrumental *glissandi* should slide for the entire written length of the note to which the glissandi/slide/bend line is attached.

ADDITIONAL BACKING TRACK

During **Night Music**, percussion 2 is instructed to play a backing track (manipulated samples of bowed crotales and nature sounds) from a CD player linked to speakers. This is to add atmosphere and a sense of physical space during the flugel horn solo. The CD is provided with the performing material.

PROFILE

Simon Dobson (b.1981) comes from Cornwall, where he began to compose in his teens. Dobson was awarded a scholarship to study composition at the Royal College of Music, London, where he studied with Timothy Salter and George Benjamin. In 2002, during his second year at the RCM, Dobson won the European Brass Band Composers' Competition with his Britten inspired work *Four Sketches*. This success led to a commission to write the set work for the 2003 Fourth Section Regional qualifying round of the National Brass Band Championships. *Lydian Pictures* has since been performed all over the world. A number of other commissions followed, including *Lyonesse* for the National Youth Brass Band Championships of Great Britain and a march for the BBC Music Live Festival. In 2004, Simon was a featured composer at the Three Choirs Festival with an electronic work entitled *Sinewave*.

In 2007, Dobson wrote the set piece for the European Brass Band Championships 'B' section. *The Drop* is based on Drum 'n' Bass techniques and its longer 'cousin' *The Drop: Remixed* has been performed a number of times in major concert venues. During his tenure as composer-in-residence with the Leyland Band, he composed a number of shorter concert works, including *The Dreaded Groove and Hook* and *Lock Horns; Rage On* and a major work *Torsion*, which received a British Composer Award nomination in 2010.

Dobson has worked with former national youth champions Mount Charles Youth Band, as well as the Devon County Youth Band and the Cornwall Youth Brass Band, for whom he wrote his most frequently played composition *Penlee*. In May 2011, the Leyland Band's recording of *Penlee* was voted in at number 106 in the Classic FM Hall of Fame. It was the highest new entry of any genre and Dobson was the seventh highest living composer in the 300-strong list. This work has been used world-wide as a test-piece in brass band competitions, including the Swiss and North American Championships.

During his residency with the Fairey Band, Dobson was commissioned to write a major work for the Stockport based band to perform at the 2011 European Brass Band Championships held in Montreux. In December 2012, this work, *A Symphony of Colours*, was only the second brass band piece to receive a British Composer Award in the 10 year history of the award up to that point. His Trombone Concerto *Shift*, written for the dynamic young virtuoso and LSO co-principal trombone Peter Moore and commissioned by the Brass Band Heritage Trust, received an acclaimed première at the 2012 RNCM Festival of Brass in Manchester. A companion concerto *Drive*, for euphonium, was premiered in 2015. Dobson also works regularly in Norway and has also forged connections with brass and wind bands in Switzerland. His Huxley inspired work *Another World's Hell* received its première performances in versions for brass, wind and fanfare bands during the 2013 Swiss Cantonale music festivals.

In 2014, Dobson's score for the British Film Institute's restoration of the 1927 epic war film *The Battles of Coronel* and *Falkland Islands* received an acclaimed première performed by the Band of Her Majesty's Royal Marines.

Away from bands, Dobson has played in the Dirty Pop band Men Of Splendour, playing to festival crowds of 10,000, and continues to compose across many different musical contemporary genres, including Drum 'n' Bass, Dub, Jazz, Breakbeat and more recently, animated film scores. Dobson has been playing trumpet and arranging for various funk/soul/jazz and hip-hop bands.

Commissioned by Nicholas Childs for the Black Dyke Band

JOURNEY OF THE LONE WOLF

1. Capturing the Peasants' Song

SIMON DOBSON

B Romanian Polka ♩ = 54 accel.

molto rit.

57
Sop. Cnt.
Solo Cnt. 1&2
Solo Cnt. 2&4
Rep. Cnt.
2nd Cnt.
3rd Cnt.
Flug.
Solo Hn
1st Hn
2nd Hn
1st Bar.
2nd Bar.
1st Tbn.
2nd Tbn.
B. Tbn.
1st Euph.
2nd Euph.
Bass E♭
Bass B♭
Timp.
Perc. 1
Perc. 2
Perc. 3 (opt.)
Perc. 4
open
gliss.
both
sec.
sim.
rim.
mf
f
fp
sfz

120
Sop. Cnt.
Solo Cnt. 1&2
Solo Cnt. 2&4
Rep. Cnt.
2nd Cnt.
3rd Cnt.
Flug.
Solo Hn
1st Hn
2nd Hn
1st Bar.
2nd Bar.
1st Tbn.
2nd Tbn.
B. Tbn.
1st Euph.
2nd Euph.
Bass E♭
Bass B♭
Timp.
Perc. 1
Perc. 2
Perc. 3 opt.
Perc. 4
open
sim.
from nothing
to Crotales
Bass drum
solo

2. Night Music

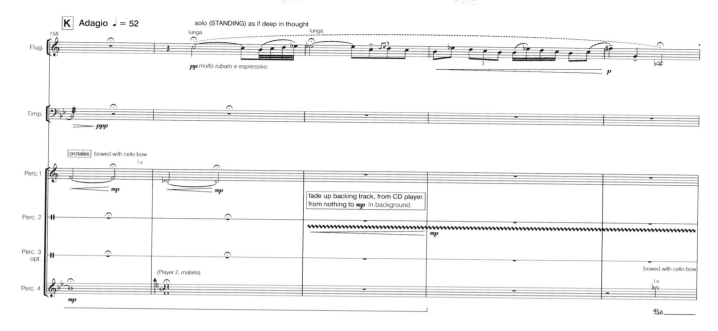

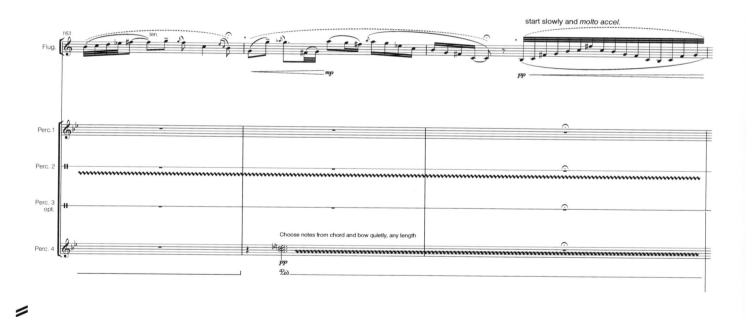

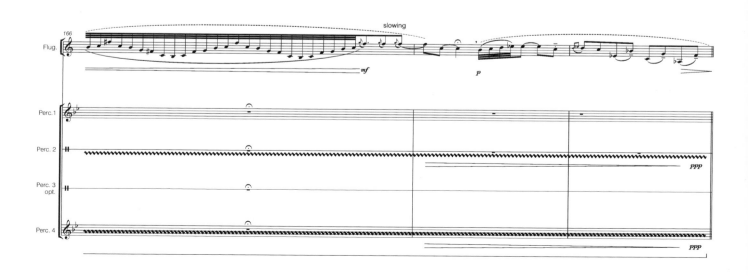

178
Sop. Cnt.
Solo Cnt. 1&2
Solo Cnt. 2&4
Rep. Cnt.
2nd Cnt.
3rd Cnt.
Flug.
Solo Hn
1st Hn
2nd Hn
1st Bar.
2nd Bar.
1st Tbn.
2nd Tbn.
B. Tbn.
1st Euph.
2nd Euph.
Bass E♭
Bass B♭
Timp.
Perc.1
Perc. 2
Perc. 3
opt.
Perc. 4
pp
p
gliss.
3

272
Sop. Cnt.
Solo Cnt. 1&2
Solo Cnt. 2&4
Rep. Cnt.
2nd Cnt.
3rd Cnt.
Flug.
Solo Hn
1st Hn
2nd Hn
1st Bar.
2nd Bar.
1st Tbn.
2nd Tbn.
B. Tbn.
1st Euph.
2nd Euph.
Bass E♭
Bass B♭
Timp.
Perc. 1
Perc. 2
Perc. 3 opt.
Perc. 4
tr
f
mf
ff
sfz
l.v

rall.

X Prestissimo ♩ = 154

307
Sop. Cnt.
Solo Cnt. 1&2
Solo Cnt. 2&4
Rep. Cnt.
2nd Cnt.
3rd Cnt.
Flug.
Solo Hn
1st Hn
2nd Hn
1st Bar.
2nd Bar.
1st Tbn.
2nd Tbn.
B. Tbn.
1st Euph.
2nd Euph.
Bass E♭
Bass B♭
Timp.
Perc. 1
Perc. 2
Perc. 3 opt.
Perc. 4
open
mf
gliss.

Y
312
Sop. Cnt.
Solo Cnt. 1&2
Solo Cnt. 2&4
Rep. Cnt.
2nd Cnt.
3rd Cnt.
Flug.
soli
Solo Hn
soli
1st Hn
soli
2nd Hn
soli
1st Bar.
2nd Bar.
1st Tbn.
gliss.
2nd Tbn.
gliss.
B. Tbn.
1st Euph.
2nd Euph.
Bass E♭
Bass B♭
Timp.
Perc. 1
Snare drum
Perc. 2
Perc. 3 opt.
Perc. 4